CONTENTS

EARLY BRIDGES

People have been building bridges across rivers and valleys for thousands of years. Cut-down trees bridged narrow streams, rope bridges spanned wider valleys and raised walkways crossed marshes.
As people learned more, they were able to build bigger bridges to carry more weight, and longer bridges to cross wider gaps.

AMAZING FACTS

In 480 BCE, King Xerxes of Persia had a 1.2 km bridge built across a narrow sea channel called the Hellespont, which is now known as the Dardanelles. He achieved this by lashing together more than 600 wooden boats.

In 580 BCE, Babylon's King Nebuchadnezzar had a stone bridge built across the River Euphrates. This joined the two parts of the city of Babylon.

The Pont du Gard, situated in the south of France, is a stone aqueduct built around 50 CE by the Romans.

SuperS

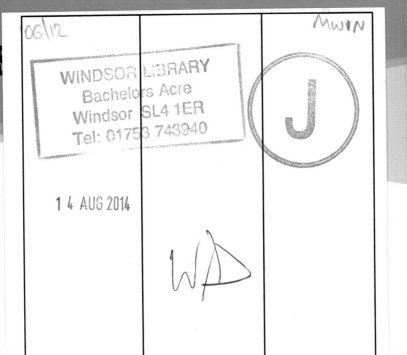

W
FRANKLIN WATTS
LONDON•SYDNEY

This edition 2012

First published in 2009 by Franklin Watts
338 Euston Road, London, NW1 3BH

Franklin Watts Australia
Hachette Children's Books
Level 17/207 Kent Street, Sydney, NSW 2000

A CIP catalogue record for this book
is available from the British Library

Dewey Classification: 624'.2

ISBN 978 1 4451 0785 1

Printed in China

Franklin Watts is a division of Hachette Children's Books, an Hachette UK company.

www.hachette.co.uk

Editor: Michael Downey
Art Direction: Harleen Mehta (Q2AMedia)
Designer: Jyotsna Julka (Q2AMedia)
Picture Researcher: Kamal Kumar (Q2AMedia)
Illustrators: Sibi N. Davasia and Danish Zaidi (Q2AMedia)

Picture credits:
t=top b=bottom c=centre l=left r=right
Cover: Carsten Reisinger/ Shutterstock: Front, Gregory James Van Raalte/ Shutterstock: Back
Title Page: Jan Zoetekouw/ Shutterstock
Elena Elisseeva/ Shutterstock: 4, Robert Estall/ Corbis: 5bl, Ian Klein/ Shutterstock: 6-7, Euchiasmus: 8,
Buzbuzzer/ iStockphoto: 9t, Christian McCarty/ Shutterstock: 10-11, Jan Zoetekouw/ Shutterstock: 12-13,
Roger Ressmeyer/ Corbis: 13br, Bettmann/ Corbis: 14, Albo/ Shutterstock: 15tr, Kevin Vertucio: 15cr,
Maureen Plainfield/ Shutterstock: 15b, Tom Carroll/ Photolibrary: 16, David R. Frazier Photolibrary, Inc./ Alamy: 17bl,
Helder Almeida/ 123rf: 18-19, Guido Alberto Rossi/ Photolibrary: 19tr, Toshitaka Morita/ Getty Images: 20,
Masanori Shiotani/ Aflo Foto Agency/ Photolibrary: 21, John Woodworth/ iStockphoto: 22,
John Maclean/ Photolibrary: 24-25, China Photos/ Stringer/ Getty Images : 26,
Xu Yu/ Associated Press: 27, Stretto Di Messina S.p.A: 28-29.

Q2AMedia Art Bank: 5r, 7t, 9b, 11t, 17c, 23, 25

Every attempt has been made to clear copyright. Should there be any inadvertent omission,
please apply to the publisher for rectification.

Note to parents and teachers:

Every effort has been made by the Publishers to ensure that the websites in this book are suitable for children, that they are of the highest educational value, and that they contain no inappropriate or offensive material. However, because of the nature of the Internet, it is impossible to guarantee that the contents of these sites will not be altered. We strongly advise that Internet access is supervised by a responsible adult.

Roman arches

Bridges were built in ancient Egypt and Greece. But the real experts in bridge building in the ancient world were the Romans, who came later. Some of their bridges are still standing, nearly 2,000 years after they were built. The Romans discovered a waterproof **concrete**, called pozzolana. This building material helped them to build strong bridge supports, or **piers**, in rivers. Using these piers, Romans built road bridges as well as bridges called **aqueducts** for carrying water.

Building from iron

Stone was the usual material for building big bridges until the 18th century. When a bridge was needed to **span** the River Severn in England, designers decided to build it from iron instead of stone. Called the Iron Bridge, this was the world's first bridge made of iron. In total, the bridge is 60 metres in length. Its longest span is 30.5 metres long. The village alongside the bridge was named Ironbridge.

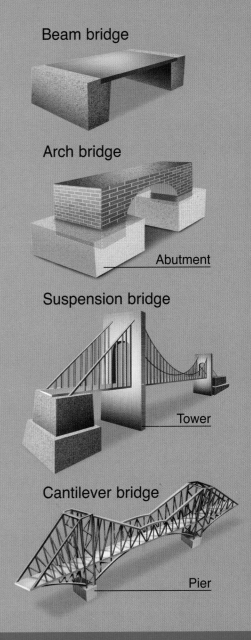

Beam bridge

Arch bridge

Abutment

Suspension bridge

Tower

Cantilever bridge

Pier

The world's first iron bridge was built across the River Severn in England in the 1770s.

BRIDGE TYPES

There are four basic types of bridge design – the beam, the arch, the suspension and the **cantilever**. A **beam bridge** is a huge slab of stone, concrete or wood that is supported at each end. The curved shape of an arched bridge can take more weight. A **suspension bridge** hangs from ropes or cables, while a **cantilever bridge** is made of beams that are supported at one end only. Today's biggest bridges are suspension bridges. Other kinds of bridges are based on these four types.

BROOKLYN BRIDGE

The Brooklyn Bridge is one of the most familiar landmarks of New York City. This suspension bridge links Manhattan with Brooklyn over the East River.

FACT FILE

- How long: 1.8 km
- Where in the world: New York City, USA
- When built: 1883
- Type of bridge: Suspension
- Designed by: John A. Roebling

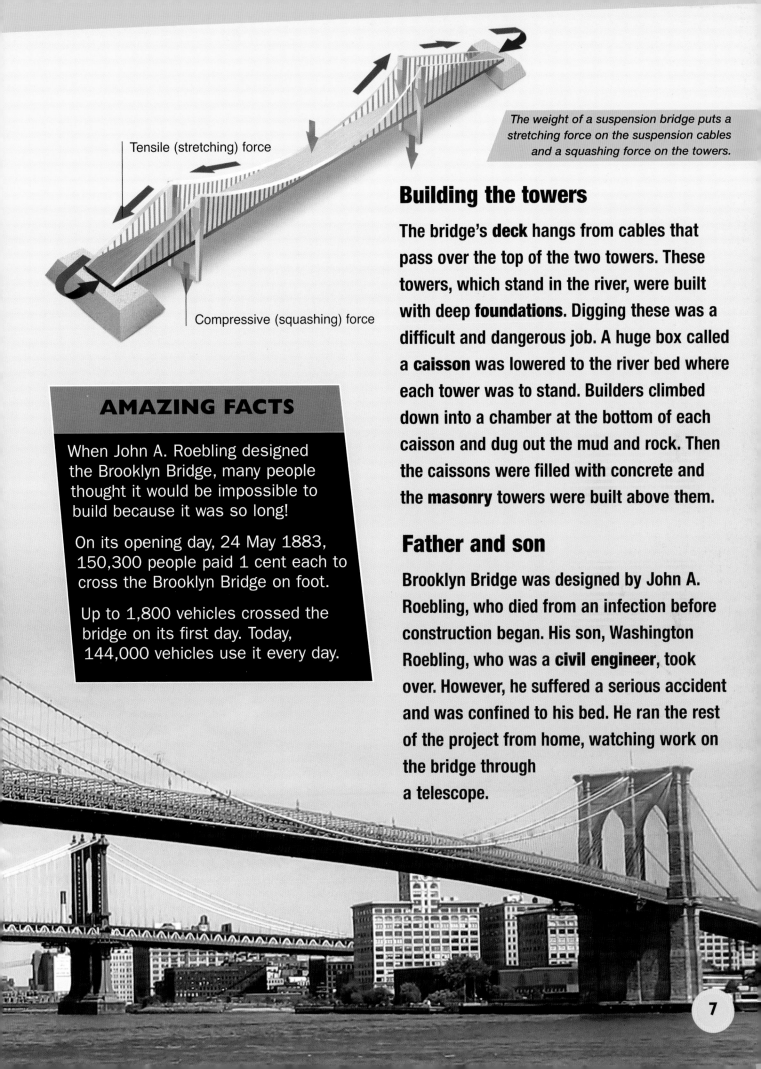

Tensile (stretching) force

Compressive (squashing) force

Building the towers

The bridge's **deck** hangs from cables that pass over the top of the two towers. These towers, which stand in the river, were built with deep **foundations**. Digging these was a difficult and dangerous job. A huge box called a **caisson** was lowered to the river bed where each tower was to stand. Builders climbed down into a chamber at the bottom of each caisson and dug out the mud and rock. Then the caissons were filled with concrete and the **masonry** towers were built above them.

Father and son

Brooklyn Bridge was designed by John A. Roebling, who died from an infection before construction began. His son, Washington Roebling, who was a **civil engineer**, took over. However, he suffered a serious accident and was confined to his bed. He ran the rest of the project from home, watching work on the bridge through a telescope.

AMAZING FACTS

When John A. Roebling designed the Brooklyn Bridge, many people thought it would be impossible to build because it was so long!

On its opening day, 24 May 1883, 150,300 people paid 1 cent each to cross the Brooklyn Bridge on foot.

Up to 1,800 vehicles crossed the bridge on its first day. Today, 144,000 vehicles use it every day.

FORTH RAIL BRIDGE

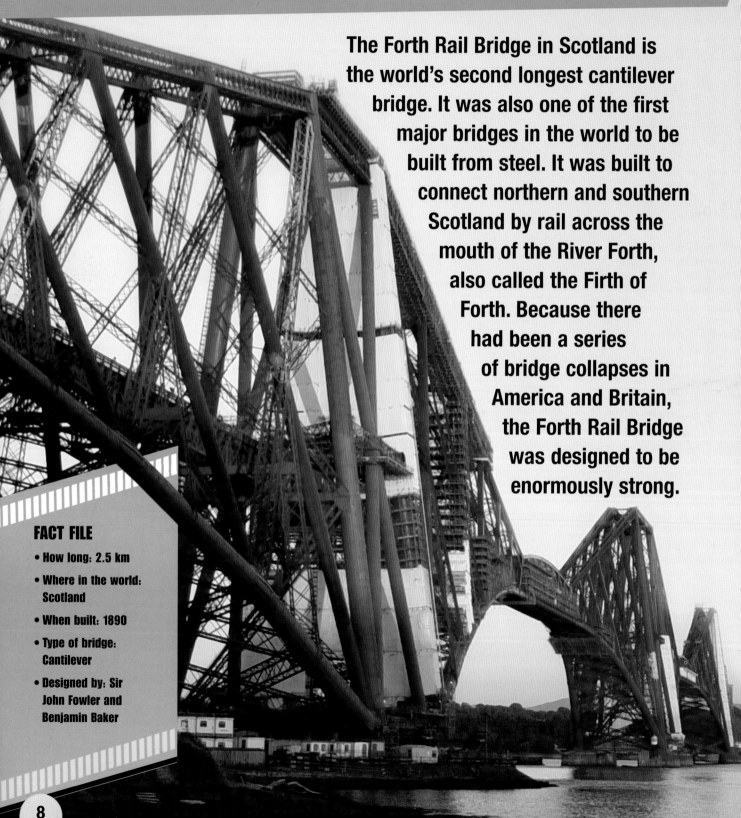

The Forth Rail Bridge in Scotland is the world's second longest cantilever bridge. It was also one of the first major bridges in the world to be built from steel. It was built to connect northern and southern Scotland by rail across the mouth of the River Forth, also called the Firth of Forth. Because there had been a series of bridge collapses in America and Britain, the Forth Rail Bridge was designed to be enormously strong.

FACT FILE

- How long: 2.5 km
- Where in the world: Scotland
- When built: 1890
- Type of bridge: Cantilever
- Designed by: Sir John Fowler and Benjamin Baker

Canada's Quebec Bridge has the longest main span of any cantilever bridge.

Bridging the depths

In the 1880s, it was common to build bridges from lots of short spans sitting on top of lines of posts called piers. Deep water made it impossible to build the Forth Rail Bridge in this way. The bridge's designers chose a different type of bridge, called a cantilever. It had only been used once before for a railway bridge built in Germany. The Forth Rail Bridge sits on three sets of piers. One set is built on an island in the river, with another set in shallow water near each shore.

Balancing act

A steel tower was built on top of each pier. Then the arms were built outwards from both sides of each tower. Building the arms on both sides of a tower at the same time balanced their weight, just like a playground see-saw. Finally, the ends of the arms were joined by short straight spans.

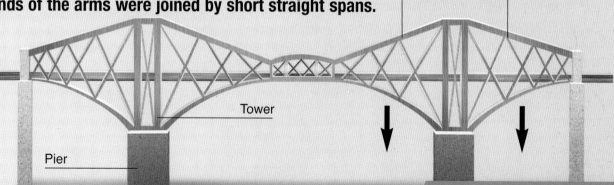

Cantilever arms

Tower

Pier

The cantilever arms on either side of a tower balance each other's weight.

WHAT IS A CANTILEVER?

A cantilever is a beam that is supported at one end only. A shelf bracket fixed to a wall and a diving board at a swimming pool are cantilevers. Big cantilever bridges were not built until the late 1800s. Until then, large bridges were made of iron. But iron cracked and broke too easily to make cantilever bridges. The production of strong, high-quality steel made cantilever bridges possible.

SYDNEY HARBOUR BRIDGE

Sydney Harbour Bridge is a steel arch bridge that spans the narrowest part of Sydney Harbour. It was modelled on the smaller Hell Gate Bridge in New York City, built in 1916. The deck, or flat surface, of an arched bridge is usually above the arch. Sydney Harbour Bridge is different. Its deck hangs below the 503-metre arch. Because of its shape, this famous Australian bridge is known as 'The Coathanger'.

Granite towers

Each half of Sydney Harbour Bridge's massive arch was built out from the shore towards the middle. Cables anchored to the ground stopped the two halves from falling into the sea until they met in the middle. Then the roadway was added and the stone towers, called **pylons**, were built at each end. The pylons hold the ends of the arch firmly in position.

FACT FILE
- How long: 1.1 km
- Where in the world: Sydney, Australia
- When built: 1932
- Type of bridge: Steel arch
- Designed by: John Bradfield and Sir Ralph Freeman

Hinge

Arch

Hinge lets the arch move

Massive hinges at each end of its steel arch allow Sydney Harbour Bridge to expand and contract without buckling.

Red-hot rivets

Most of the steel used to build Sydney Harbour Bridge was made in England and shipped halfway around the world to Sydney. The granite was quarried at Moruya on the south coast of New South Wales in Australia. The steel parts were lifted into position and fastened together with pins called rivets. These rivets were heated until they were red-hot, then thrown up to rivet catchers on the bridge who hammered them in place.

BRIDGE EXPANSION

Bridges expand or contract when the temperature changes. To prevent them from cracking up, expansion joints are built into most bridges. Sydney Harbour Bridge, however, has giant hinges at the ends of the main arch that do the same job. These hinges absorb up-and-down movements of up to 18 centimetres in the arch as it warms or cools.

GOLDEN GATE BRIDGE

The Golden Gate Bridge is one of the most famous bridges in the world. It is a suspension bridge that spans the Golden Gate, the opening into San Francisco Bay from the Pacific Ocean. When it was completed in 1937, it became the world's longest suspension bridge. The Golden Gate Bridge held this record for nearly 30 years.

FACT FILE

- How long: 2.7 km
- Where in the world: San Francisco, USA
- When built: 1937
- Type of bridge: Suspension
- Designed by: Charles Ellis, Irving Morrow and Leon Moisseiff

Choosing a colour

The most noticeable thing about the Golden Gate Bridge is its colour. The bridge is painted a colour called international orange, or orange vermillion. It was chosen by **architect** Irving Morrow to make the bridge blend in with the red hillsides. It also makes the bridge easier to see in the Golden Gate's thick fog. A team of painters continually maintain the paintwork.

Earthquake damage

In San Francisco, earthquakes are common. Most of them are small tremors, but major earthquakes have struck the area and will do so again. Since the Golden Gate Bridge was built, engineers have learned a lot more about how earthquakes affect bridges. When they realised that the Golden Gate Bridge could be damaged by a strong earthquake, engineering work to strengthen it was ordered. The construction project is underway and will proceed in two phases, stretching over several years.

AMAZING FACTS

The Golden Gate Bridge weighs 804,700 tonnes. Its towers, which weigh 40,200 tonnes each, are held together by 600,000 rivets.

The bridge is crossed by 40 million vehicles every year.

The Golden Gate Bridge has appeared in many films, including *X-Men: The Last Stand, Star Trek VI: The Undiscovered Country, Star Trek IV: The Voyage Home, Superman* and the James Bond film *A View to a Kill*.

A team of 38 painters look after the bridge's paintwork; 17 ironworkers replace corroded steel and rivets.

Building the bridge

Construction work on the Golden Gate Bridge began in 1933. The first job was to build the piers that its towers stand on. The north pier was built in shallow water with no difficulty. The south pier was more difficult as it had to be built 335 metres from the shore in water 30 metres deep. It was the first bridge pier to be built in the open ocean. First, a wall called a **fender** was built to protect the pier from being hit by ships. Then concrete was poured inside it and the pier was built on top.

AMAZING FACTS

Each of the Golden Gate Bridge's two main suspension cables can support a weight of 56,000 tonnes.

The main suspension cables contain 129,000 km of wire, enough to go around the world more than three times!

Workers started removing the bridge's original paint in 1965 and replacing it with a more modern paint. The task took 30 years to complete.

Suspension cables

To save on weight, the bridge's towers were made of steel rather than brick, stone and concrete. More weight was saved by making them hollow. The suspension cables were strung from one end of the bridge to the other over the tops of the towers. Each cable contains 27,572 wires, each one as thick as a pencil. The ends of the cables are held firmly by enormous concrete **anchor blocks**. Each block weighs over 45,000 tonnes. This is heavier than a battleship!

Safety net

The Golden Gate Bridge set new safety standards in bridge building. A safety net was used for the first time. The rope net was hung underneath the bridge when work on the deck began. During four years of construction work, the net caught 19 workers who fell. They would probably have died without it.

The Golden Gate Bridge's main suspension cables are made up of thousands of wires.

The Golden Gate Bridge's deck is reinforced by many interlocking steel girders. They add strength and also let the wind blow through.

LAKE PONTCHARTRAIN CAUSEWAY

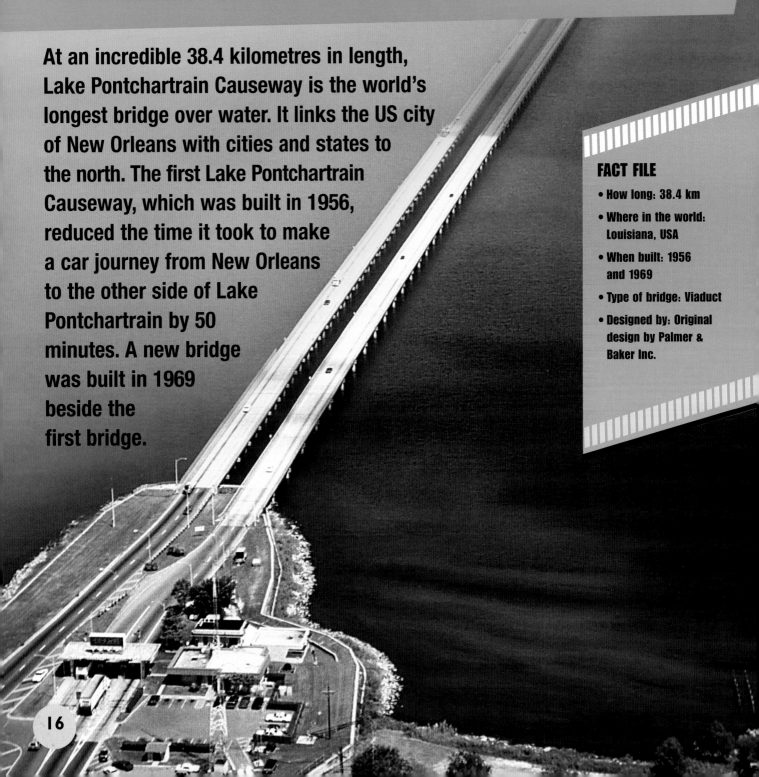

At an incredible 38.4 kilometres in length, Lake Pontchartrain Causeway is the world's longest bridge over water. It links the US city of New Orleans with cities and states to the north. The first Lake Pontchartrain Causeway, which was built in 1956, reduced the time it took to make a car journey from New Orleans to the other side of Lake Pontchartrain by 50 minutes. A new bridge was built in 1969 beside the first bridge.

FACT FILE

- How long: 38.4 km
- Where in the world: Louisiana, USA
- When built: 1956 and 1969
- Type of bridge: Viaduct
- Designed by: Original design by Palmer & Baker Inc.

Driving the piles

Lake Pontchartrain Causeway sits on 9,500 hollow concrete tubes, or **piles**, which form a firm base for the roadway. These piles were driven into the lake bed, with the deepest going down more than 20 metres. The roadway was made in sections on the shore. These sections were floated out on **barges** and lifted into position on top of the piles.

Room for ships

For most of the bridge's length, the roadway is only about 4.5 metres above the water. To allow small ships and boats to pass underneath, the designers built three humps into the bridge. The roadway gently rises to a height of 15 metres above the water at the top of the biggest hump. To let bigger ships pass through, a drawbridge, also called a **bascule**, can lift up part of the roadway 13 kilometres from the north shore.

The causeway is a long chain of beam bridges. To cope with the compression and stretching caused by traffic, pre-stressed concrete was used.

Weight of traffic pushes down

Top of section is compressed

Pre-stressed concrete

Bottom of section is stretched

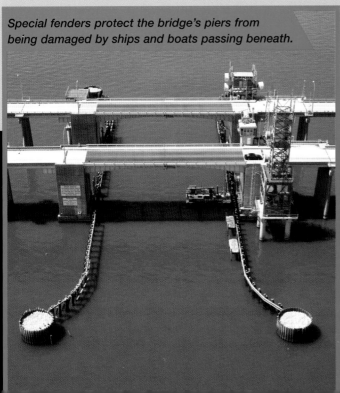

Special fenders protect the bridge's piers from being damaged by ships and boats passing beneath.

STRONG CONCRETE

Concrete can be strengthened by putting steel rods, called **rebars**, inside it. This is known as reinforced concrete. Pre-stressed concrete is even stronger. Wires, called tendons, are put inside the concrete while it is wet. These wires are then stretched. The concrete sets hard with the stretched tendons inside it. Lake Pontchartrain Causeway was one of the world's first bridges to be built from pre-stressed concrete.

VASCO DA GAMA BRIDGE

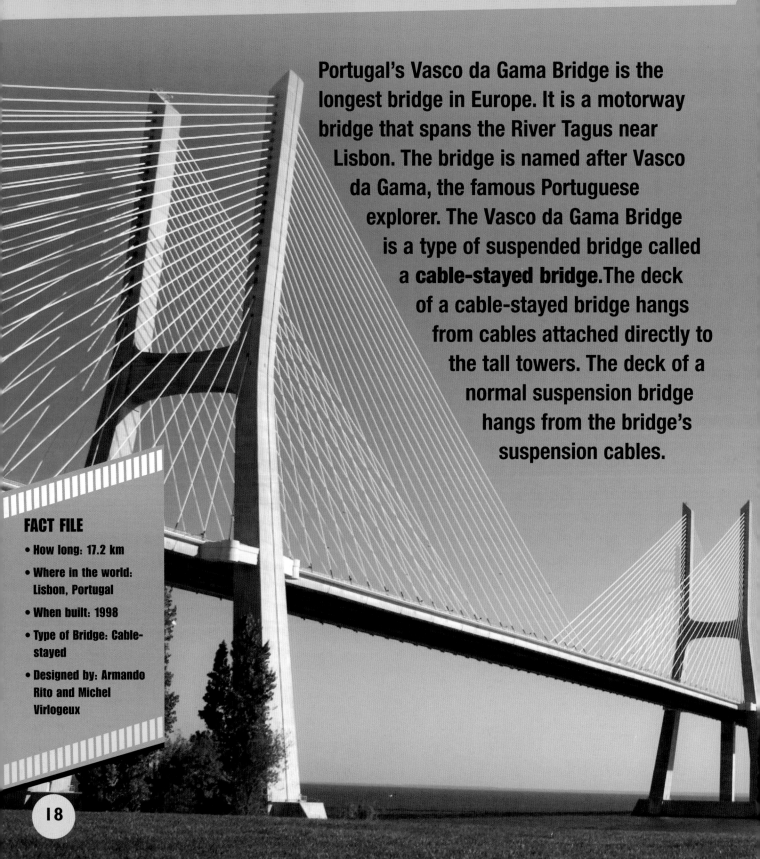

Portugal's Vasco da Gama Bridge is the longest bridge in Europe. It is a motorway bridge that spans the River Tagus near Lisbon. The bridge is named after Vasco da Gama, the famous Portuguese explorer. The Vasco da Gama Bridge is a type of suspended bridge called a **cable-stayed bridge**. The deck of a cable-stayed bridge hangs from cables attached directly to the tall towers. The deck of a normal suspension bridge hangs from the bridge's suspension cables.

FACT FILE

- How long: 17.2 km
- Where in the world: Lisbon, Portugal
- When built: 1998
- Type of Bridge: Cable-stayed
- Designed by: Armando Rito and Michel Virlogeux

Two tall towers

The cable-stayed section of the bridge spans 825 metres of the bridge's 17.2 kilometre length. The deck here is held up by cables hanging from two tall towers. In this part of the bridge, the deck rises gently to 45 metres above the sea at high tide so that ships can sail underneath. The rest of the Vasco da Gama Bridge is a **viaduct**, which is the name given to a bridge made up of many short spans.

Surviving earthquakes

As Portugal has suffered serious earthquakes in the past, the Vasco da Gama Bridge had to be specially designed so that it would not collapse during an earthquake. On 1 November 1755, Portugal was hit by one of the worst earthquakes in history. This massive earthquake destroyed Lisbon and sent a huge wave, called a tsunami, sweeping across the coasts of Portugal, Spain and Morocco. It was a terrible disaster in which 60,000 people died. The Vasco da Gama Bridge has been designed to survive an earthquake more than four times worse than the 1755 'quake.

The bridge's slender H-shaped towers soar to a height of 150 metres. These towers carry the cables that support the roadway.

AMAZING FACTS

The Vasco da Gama Bridge was built in only 18 months so that it could open in time to carry tourists to the Expo '98 World's Fair in Lisbon.

The bridge is so long that its designers had to take account of the curved shape of the Earth's surface.

The bridge's elegant towers stand on piles that go down 95 metres below sea level.

AKASHI–KAIKYO BRIDGE

The Akashi–Kaikyo Bridge is the world's longest and highest suspension bridge. Its centre span is 1,991 metres long, the biggest of any suspension bridge built so far. It spans the Akashi Strait, a busy shipping seaway between the Japanese islands of Honshu and Shikoku. About 1,400 ships pass through the **strait** every day. The bridge's designers had to make the main span long and high enough so that they could pass safely underneath.

FACT FILE

- How long: 3.9 km
- Where in the world: Japan
- When built: 1998
- Type of bridge: Suspension
- Designed by: Honshu–Shikoku Bridge Authority

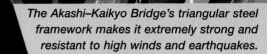
The Akashi–Kaikyo Bridge's triangular steel framework makes it extremely strong and resistant to high winds and earthquakes.

Crashing waves

The bridge's designers faced a difficult challenge. Somehow, they had to create a giant bridge that could stand up to the strong sea currents flowing around it. They also had to deal with big waves crashing against it, strong winds trying to blow it over and earthquakes trying to shake it to bits! To make their task even more difficult, this massive structure had to be built in water 110 metres deep.

Triangles for strength

The bridge's deck uses a traditional design common in the USA. It sits on top of a frame of steel girders linked together in triangles, called **trusses**. The truss makes the deck strong, but also lets the wind blow through. The deck was built in sections. The sections were floated out to the bridge on barges and hoisted into position 65 metres above the water.

AMAZING FACTS

The Akashi–Kaikyo Bridge is one metre longer than it was meant to be. This is because an earthquake moved its two towers a metre further apart while it was being built!

The bridge's suspension cables contain 300,000 km of wire. This is enough to go around the Earth more than seven times.

The main span is 710 metres longer than the Golden Gate Bridge's main span.

MILLAU VIADUCT

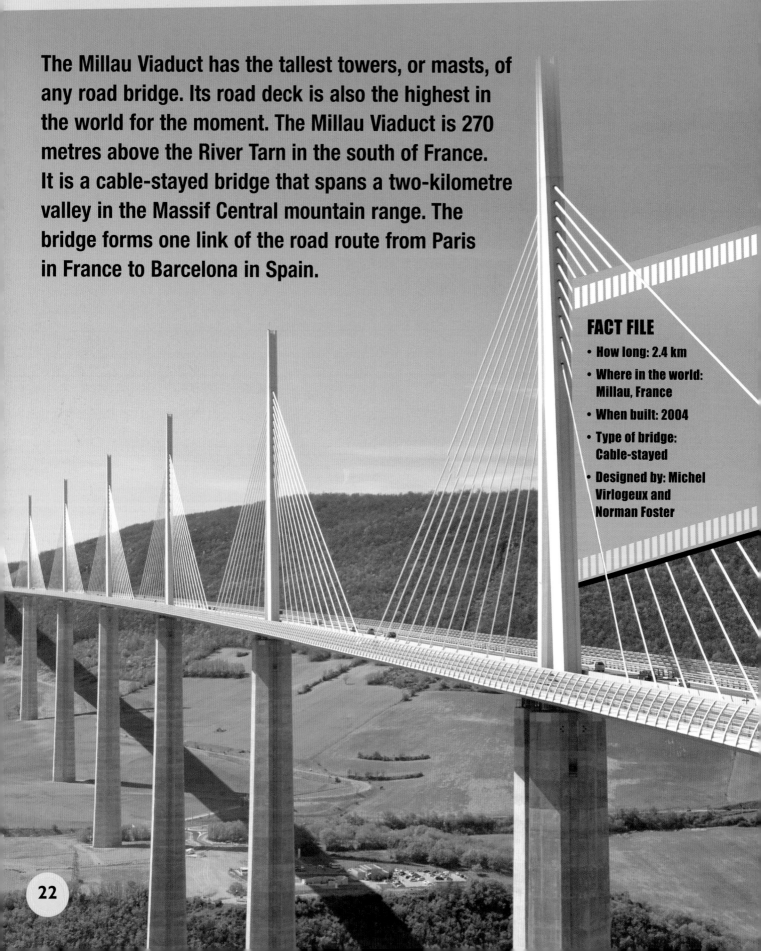

The Millau Viaduct has the tallest towers, or masts, of any road bridge. Its road deck is also the highest in the world for the moment. The Millau Viaduct is 270 metres above the River Tarn in the south of France. It is a cable-stayed bridge that spans a two-kilometre valley in the Massif Central mountain range. The bridge forms one link of the road route from Paris in France to Barcelona in Spain.

FACT FILE

- How long: 2.4 km
- Where in the world: Millau, France
- When built: 2004
- Type of bridge: Cable-stayed
- Designed by: Michel Virlogeux and Norman Foster

See-through bridge

The usual way to span a valley with a suspension bridge, or a cable-stayed bridge, would be to hang the roadway from two massive towers. The Millau Viaduct's designers decided to do something different. They searched for a way to make the bridge look as delicate and see-through as possible. They came up with a design that makes the Millau Viaduct one of the most elegant and graceful bridges in the world.

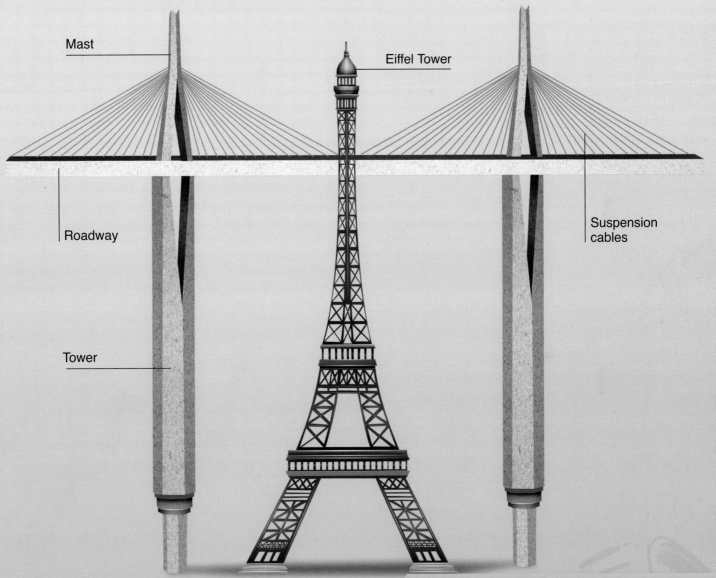

Mast

Eiffel Tower

Roadway

Suspension cables

Tower

The top of the Millau Viaduct's tallest mast is 343 metres high. This is about 19 metres higher than the Eiffel Tower.

Seven elegant masts

Famous British architect Norman Foster was in charge of the bridge's appearance. Instead of the usual two towers, the roadway is held up by cables hanging from the tops of seven tall, slim masts. Each section between a pair of masts spans 342 metres. In addition, the bridge uses the minimum amount of material, as well as the lightest materials possible. The deck, masts and cables are all made of steel.

Moulding the towers

To make a firm foundation for the Millau Viaduct, piles were sunk deep into the ground. The towers were then constructed on top of these. A mould, called shuttering or **formwork**, was built around the top of the piles and concrete poured in. When the concrete had set hard, the formwork was pushed up higher and more concrete was poured in. This continued until each tower reached the correct height.

Launching the deck

The deck of a new bridge is usually lifted into position by a huge crane. But when the Millau Viaduct was built, engineers used a different method. Each half of the deck was slid out from either end of the bridge towards the middle. Sliding the deck out from the end of a bridge like this is called 'launching the deck'.

AMAZING FACTS

Each of the 22 cables that hang from the top of every mast is made of 91 strands. Each one of these strands contains seven steel wires.

A new type of flexible bitumen was developed to make the viaduct's roadway. Bitumen is a black, sticky material like tar. It lets the metal deck bend as traffic passes over it without cracking the road surface.

When the bridge was built, hundreds of instruments were added to it to record the way it bends or shakes due to wind or traffic.

Hoisting the masts

While the viaduct was being erected, temporary steel towers were built between the permanent concrete towers. Then the two halves of the deck were joined together in the middle. After this, tall masts were placed on top of the towers. These were driven out on to the deck in pieces, welded together and lifted into position. Cables were connected to the top of each mast to hold up the deck. Then the temporary towers were taken down. To reduce the speed of the wind blowing across the roadway, sidescreens were fitted to the deck.

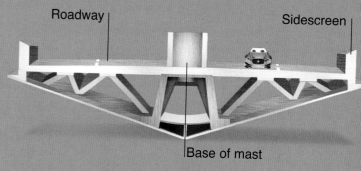

The Millau Viaduct's slender steel deck carries a four-lane roadway, with two lanes in each direction.

Roadway

Sidescreen

Base of mast

Mast

Cable

Sliding deck

Roadway

Tower

Temporary tower

During construction work, temporary towers supported the roadway while deck sections were slid out towards the next concrete tower.

HANGZHOU BAY BRIDGE

The Hangzhou Bay Bridge is the world's longest ocean-crossing bridge. It links China's biggest city, Shanghai, with the city of Ningbo across Hangzhou Bay, on the east coast of China. It cuts the distance by road between the two cities by 120 kilometres, which will reduce journey time by one hour. It also brings Ningbo's port, China's second largest cargo port, within easy reach of Shanghai.

FACT FILE

- How long: 35.7 km
- Where in the world: China
- When built: 2007
- Type of bridge: Cable-stayed plus viaducts
- Designed by: Ty Lin International

Wall of water

Hangzhou Bay is one of the most difficult places on Earth to build a bridge. When the tide comes in, the shape of the bay changes the tide into a wall of water up to 8 metres high travelling at 30 km/h. This mass of water is called a 'tidal bore'. Hangzhou Bay has the world's biggest tidal bore. Tropical storms, or typhoons, also sweep through the bay. It took nine years of research and more than 120 technical studies involving more than 600 experts to plan how to build a stable bridge under these challenging conditions.

Cable-stayed spans

The greater part of Hangzhou Bay Bridge is made of short spans sitting on top of piers anchored to the sea bed. Two parts of the bridge, however, are cable-stayed. The northern cable-stayed span is 448 metres long and the southern span is 318 metres long. These cable-stayed spans have no supports below the deck, so that ships can sail underneath. Some parts of the bridge were so big and heavy that no existing bridge-building machine in the world could handle them. New machines had to be specially built.

AMAZING FACTS

The Hangzhou Bay Bridge was built from a staggering 2.45 million tonnes of concrete and 800,000 tonnes of steel by 20 construction teams of 5,000 workers.

A giant truck with 640 wheels was built to move parts of the bridge.

The bridge is designed to carry up to 100,000 vehicles a day.

The total cost of the bridge's construction came to a massive $1.7 billion.

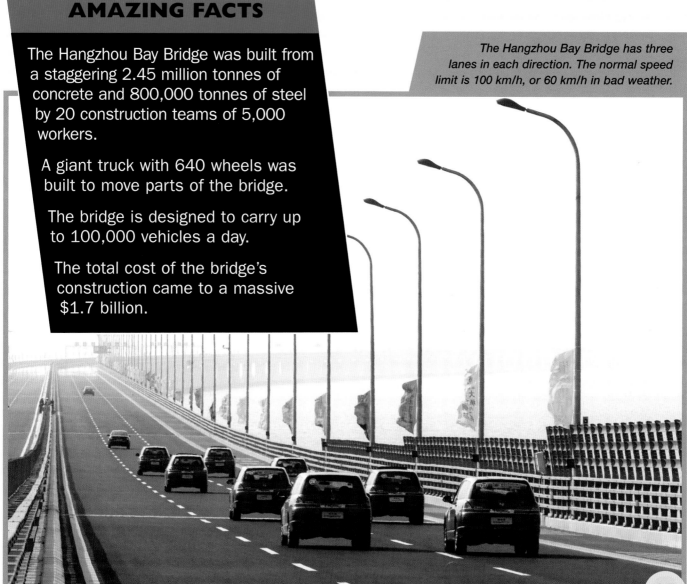

The Hangzhou Bay Bridge has three lanes in each direction. The normal speed limit is 100 km/h, or 60 km/h in bad weather.

BRIDGES IN THE FUTURE

As scientists and engineers learn more about bridges and their strengths and weaknesses, they find ways of building bridges that seemed impossible just a few years ago. Each new record-breaking bridge pushes the science and engineering a little further.

Spanning the world

A new record-breaking bridge is being planned between two Gulf states, Qatar and Bahrain. Its unofficial name is the Qatar-Bahrain Friendship Bridge and it will open in 2015 or later. Up to 45 kilometres long, it will be the world's longest **fixed link** when completed. There are also plans to build bridges from Italy to Sicily across the Messina Strait, from Europe to Africa across the Strait of Gibraltar and even from the USA to Russia across the Bering Strait.

Latest technology

In the past, when bridges were designed using **slide rules** and drawing paper, something occasionally went wrong. The Tay Bridge in Scotland collapsed in 1879. It was made of iron, which broke up in strong winds as a train crossed it. The Tacoma Narrows Bridge in the USA collapsed in 1940 when its thin, lightweight deck twisted so much in the wind that it shattered. Bridges are far safer today, and will be even safer in the future, because their designs are tested using the latest technology.

AMAZING FACTS

A bridge across the Bering Strait would have to cope with freezing winter temperatures as low as –50 °C.

The Qatar–Bahrain Friendship Bridge will cut the journey time by car between the two states from five hours to only 30 minutes.

When the Strait of Messina Bridge is built, it will be the world's longest suspension bridge. Its main span will be twice the length of today's record holder, the Akashi–Kaikyo Bridge.

An artist's impression of the proposed Strait of Messina Bridge, which will link Italy and Sicily.

GLOSSARY

anchor blocks
massive blocks of stone or concrete that hold the ends of a suspension bridge's main suspension cables in place

aqueduct
bridge that carries water across a valley

architect
professional designer of buildings and other structures, including bridges

barge
flat-bottomed boat for moving large, heavy cargoes such as parts of bridges

bascule
type of bridge, or part of a bridge, with a deck that opens upwards

beam bridge
simple bridge made by supporting a tree trunk, stone slab or concrete beam at each end

cable-stayed bridge
type of suspended bridge with a deck held up by cables attached to the tops of tall towers called pylons or masts

caisson
large tank, open at the bottom, used to build bridge foundations. A caisson is sunk to the river bed. Water is pumped out. Workmen enter the caisson and dig down until they reach solid rock. Then the caisson

is filled with concrete to form the foundation of one of the bridge's piers

cantilever
beam held at one end only

cantilever bridge
type of bridge made with cantilevers, which are beams that are supported at one end only

causeway
road raised above water

civil engineer
an engineer who works primarily with construction projects in public places. These include office buildings, bridges and roads

concrete
construction material made from a mixture of sand, gravel, cement and water that can be moulded into any shape and sets as hard as rock

deck
part of a bridge that cars or trains are driven along

fender
wall built around a bridge pier to protect it from being hit by ships

fixed link
bridge or tunnel, or a combination of the two, that permanently connects two places

formwork
temporary mould that concrete is poured into until it sets hard

foundations
solid underground structure on which a building, such as a bridge, stands. A bridge's foundations always extend many metres below ground

masonry
structure built from bricks or stones cemented together

pier
one of the supports that bears the weight of a bridge

pile
beam made of wood, steel or concrete driven into the ground to carry a heavy load, such as a bridge

pylons
tall towers that support a bridge's cables or arch

rebars
reinforcing bars, or steel rods, inside concrete to make it stronger. Concrete strengthened with rebars is called reinforced concrete

rivets
metal pins used to fasten the parts of bridges, and other structures, together

slide rule
ruler with sliding parts that can be used to do simple calculations

span
distance between two supports of a bridge. The main span is the longest of these distances

strait
narrow channel linking two larger bodies of water

suspension bridge
bridge with a deck that hangs from thick cables supported by towers

truss
frame made of wood, iron or steel beams linked together to make a strong, lightweight structure

viaduct
long bridge made from lots of short spans, carrying a road or railway across land or water

INDEX

WEBLINKS

http://science.howstuffworks.com/engineering/civil/bridge.htm
An introduction to bridges of all kinds and how they work.

www.goldengatebridge.org/research/facts.php
Answers to all of your questions about the Golden Gate Bridge.

www.sydneyharbourbridge.info
The history and construction of the Sydney Harbour Bridge.

www.forthbridges.org.uk/railbridgemain.htm
The history and construction of the Forth Rail Bridge.

www.pbs.org/wgbh/buildingbig/wonder/structure/akashi_kaikyo.html
Discover more about the world's longest bridge.